MW01250730

Welcome to the Olympics

by Meish Goldish
illustrated by Tim Jones

SCHOOL PUBLISHERS

Printed in China

ISBN 10: 0-15-351169-9
ISBN 13: 978-0-15-351169-1

Ordering Options
ISBN 10: 0-15-350603-2 (Grade 6 On-Level Collection)
ISBN 13: 978-0-15-350603-1 (Grade 6 On-Level Collection)
ISBN 10: 0-15-358002-X (package of 5)
ISBN 13: 978-0-15-358002-4 (package of 5)

4 5 6 7 8 9 10   0940   12 11 10 09

Characters

Sportscaster

Team Coach

Javelin Thrower

Discus Thrower

Long Jumper

Sprinter

Wrestler

Chariot Racer

Sportscaster: Good afternoon, ladies and gentlemen. I'm glad you're time-traveling with me to the 676 B.C. Olympic Games. I'm standing here in the Stadium of Olympia in western Greece. In our pre-games show, I'll be interviewing athletes who will be competing this year. However, let's first talk with one of the team coaches. Good afternoon, sir.

Team Coach: Good afternoon, madam. It's a pleasure to promote the Olympics on your show today.

Sportscaster: Can you tell us a little about this year's Olympic Games?

Team Coach: I'd be happy to. As you know, this year marks the hundredth anniversary of the games, which began in 776 B.C. The games are held every four years, so this is the twenty-fifth meeting. And I'm very happy to say that they're still flourishing nicely.

Sportscaster: Have the Olympics changed much in those one hundred years?

Team Coach: Yes. In the twenty-five games that preceded ours, there were fewer events. In fact, at the first Olympics there was only one event, the 200-yard (183 m) footrace. In this Olympics, we have many more events. The games are much more sophisticated.

Sportscaster: How did the Olympics get started?

Team Coach: The games began as a way to honor our Greek god Zeus. As everyone knows, he's the king of all the other Greek gods. He's quite an imposing figure.

Sportscaster: Who can we expect to see in this year's Olympics?

Team Coach: The athletes have come from all over Greece. You'll see a lot of young men from Sparta and Athens. Those two Greek cities have battled for years over which is stronger. It's better they decide by playing games than by pillaging each other's towns and taking away the treasures.

Sportscaster: Thank you for spending time with us today. Now I see an athlete nearby. Excuse me, sir, who are you?

Javelin Thrower: I'm a proud Spartan. I'll be part of the javelin throwing contest.

Sportscaster: What is a javelin, exactly?

Javelin Thrower: It's a long, straight spear with a sharp point at one end.

Sportscaster: How do you throw it?

Javelin Thrower: Well, I run up to the line at the front of the stadium. Then I release it from a leather strap that is attached to the javelin.

Sportscaster: How far can you throw it?

Javelin Thrower: Last year, I threw a javelin almost 260 feet (79.2 m).

Sportscaster: Wow, you must be greatly revered for accomplishing such a feat. That's nearly as long as a football field!

Javelin Thrower: What's a football field?

Sportscaster: Oh, I forgot. The game of football won't be invented for about another 2,500 years. Thank you for your time. Now here's another athlete. Who are you?

Discus Thrower: I throw the discus for the Athens team. Athenians rule! We'll be immortalized forever after we win here this year!

Sportscaster: What is a discus?

Discus Thrower: It's a round plate made of metal or stone. It weighs about five pounds (2.3 kg).

Sportscaster: That's heavy. How far can you throw it?

Discus Thrower: My best throw ever was just over 200 feet (61 m).

Sportscaster: How do you manage to throw it so far?

Discus Thrower: I hold the discus in the palm of my hand. My fingertips are curled around the rim. I whirl around to gain speed and power. Then I let go and watch it soar!

Sportscaster: That sounds pretty much the same as it is thrown today.

Discus Thrower: What do you mean?

Sportscaster: I mean—that sounds like a challenge. Good luck in the games. Now we have another athlete here. Who are you?

Long Jumper: I'm a long jumper for Sparta. I see how far I can leap across a sand pit.

Sportscaster: What's the farthest you've jumped?

Long Jumper: My best jump ever was twenty feet two inches (6.1 m). That's a record befitting a champion, if I do say so myself!

Sportscaster: Goodness, that's quite a feat!

Long Jumper: That's correct, but it's not that difficult for me to leap so far. I carry weights called *halteres* in my hands and swing my arms to propel me forward. You'd be surprised by how far I can soar. Most people couldn't land from such a distance intact, but I do. I am the greatest!

Sportscaster: You're not exactly unassuming, are you? So do you use the *halteres* when you train?

Long Jumper: Of course! I use them on practice jumps, and also lift them to build up my arm muscles in between jumps.

Sportscaster: They look heavy. What are they made of?

Long Jumper: Some *halteres* are made of lead, but I like these stone ones better. Now if you'll excuse me, I have to keep practicing.

Sportscaster: Oh, of course. Good luck to you! Now I see another athlete running near me. Who are you?

Sprinter: I'm a sprinter for the Spartans. I take part in the shorter running races. I run at full speed the whole time.

Sportscaster: How fast can you run?

Sprinter: I've done the *stade* in just thirty seconds, and the *diaulos* in sixty-seven seconds.

Sportscaster: Now how long are the stade and diaulos?

Sprinter: The *stade* is one lap around the stadium and the *diaulos* is two.

Sportscaster: That sounds pretty fast. Are there other types of running races in the Olympics?

Sprinter: There is the *dolichos*, which is a long distance race. There is also a race in which the runners wear a helmet and carry a shield.

Sportscaster: Do you run the marathon, too?

Sprinter: What's the marathon? Do you mean Marathon the city?

Sportscaster: I forgot, that race hasn't been created yet.

Sportscaster: It must take a lot of training to get into shape for your runs.

Sprinter: Oh, yes, I train the entire year. Only the most notable Greek athletes are allowed to compete in the Olympic Games. After all, we want to honor Zeus with only the best.

Sportscaster: That's certainly true. Now I have another athlete standing before me. Who are you?

Wrestler: I'm on the Athens wrestling team. My goal is to pin those ornery Spartans to the ground in a very short time. I want to make Zeus and my grandfather proud.

Sportscaster: Was your grandfather an Olympic wrestler like you?

Wrestler: No, he worked on a farm with fertile soil and wrestled his friends when there was no work. He always wanted to participate in the games. He was aggravated because wrestling didn't become an Olympic sport until 708 B.C. That was just thirty-two years ago. I'm the first member of my family to wrestle in the games.

Sportscaster: What's the key to good wrestling?

Wrestler: The main thing is to be fast. According to Olympic rules, you can use your legs to trip or tackle your opponent. As a result, I must be overwhelming with my strong legs.

Sportscaster: Good luck in your match today. Now I see one final athlete to talk with. Who are you?

Chariot Racer: I'm a Spartan chariot racer.

Sportscaster: What is a chariot, exactly?

Chariot Racer: It's a wooden cart that's pulled by horses. They just added four-horse chariot racing to the Olympic Games four years ago. This is my first time riding.

Sportscaster: Do you sit atop one of the horses?

Chariot Racer: Goodness, no! I sit in the cart and control the horses with reins. Those are the straps that tell the horses to run faster or slower. I influence the horses' speed by what I do with the reins.

Sportscaster: Sort of like the driver controls a car with the gas pedal and brake, right?

Chariot Racer: What's a gas pedal and brake? What's a car?

Sportscaster: Oops, I keep forgetting. I'm just visiting here from the future. I guess I've made myself pretty conspicuous by now.

Chariot Racer: What time in the future do you live?

Sportscaster: Nearly 2,700 years from now.

Chariot Racer: Hah! I'll bet you don't have Olympic Games in your day.

Sportscaster: You'd be surprised, believe me. Well, I want to thank everyone who took part in my show today. I hope all of you are prosperous and win gold medals this year.

Team Coach: Gold medals? The winners in these Olympic Games win a crown of leaves to wear upon their heads.

Sportscaster: Then wear them proudly! Good-bye!

Think Critically

1. Name at least five events in the ancient Olympic Games.

2. How were the Olympic Games in 676 B.C. different from the first Olympic Games ever held?

3. Which ancient Olympic sport in the story seems most difficult to you? Explain.

4. Why was each athlete in the games so determined to do well and win?

5. Why was it unusual that the Sportscaster was able to interview the Olympic athletes in the story?

 Social Studies

More on Ancient Greece Research another aspect of ancient Greece. Consider government or geography. Summarize your findings.

School-Home Connection Summarize for your family the Readers' Theater you read. Invite family members to each name their favorite competitive sport and explain why they like it.